best
easy
day hikes
Lake Tahoe

Tracy Salcedo

FALCON®

HELENA, MONTANA

*A*FALCONGUIDE®

Falcon® Publishing is continually expanding its list of recreational guidebooks. All books include detailed descriptions, accurate maps, and all information necessary for enjoyable trips. You can order extra copies of this book and get information and prices for other Falcon® books by writing Falcon, P.O. Box 1718, Helena, MT 59624 or calling toll free 1-800-582-2665. Also, please ask for a free copy of our current catalog. Visit our website at www.FalconOutdoors.com or contact us by e-mail at falcon@falconguide.com.

© 1999 Falcon® Publishing, Inc., Helena, Montana.
Printed in Canada.

1 2 3 4 5 6 7 8 9 0 TP 04 03 02 01 00 99

Falcon and FalconGuide are registered trademarks of Falcon® Publishing, Inc.

Library of Congress Cataloguing-in-Publication Data
Salcedo, Tracy.
  Best easy day hikes, Lake Tahoe / Tracy Salcedo.
      p.   cm. — (A Falcon guide)
  ISBN 1-56044-866-0 (pbk.)
      1. Hiking—Tahoe, Lake, Region (Calif. and Nev.)—Guidebooks.
  2. Tahoe, Lake, Region (Calif. and Nev.)—Guidebooks.   I. Title.
  II. Series.
  GV199.42.T16S35   1999
  917.94'38—dc21   99-19751
                                                        CIP

CAUTION

Outdoor recreational activities are by their very nature potentially hazardous. All participants in such activities must assume responsibility for their own actions and safety. The information contained in this guidebook cannot replace sound judgment and good decision-making skills, which help reduce risk exposure, nor does the scope of this book allow for disclosure of all the potential hazards and risks involved in such activities.

Learn as much as possible about the outdoor recreational activities in which you participate, prepare for the unexpected, and be cautious. The reward will be a safer and more enjoyable experience.

 Text pages printed on recycled paper.

*This book is dedicated to the
Friedman and Rodman families.*

Acknowledgments

Thanks to the following folk for their advice, help, and generosity: Mike St. Michel and Don Lane of the USDA Forest Service–Lake Tahoe Basin Management Unit; Dave Nettle of Alpenglow Sports in Tahoe City; Gisela Steiner of Tahoe Trail Trekkers; the folks who have worked long and hard to create the wonderful Tahoe Rim Trail; the friendly and helpful local people I met on the trail; Bill Schneider for his thoughtful introductory material; editors David Lee, Charlene Patterson and Erica Olsen; Howard and Rita Friedman and their family; Jesse and Judy Salcedo for hike scouting (and so much more); Angela Jones; Chris Salcedo; George Meyers; my awesome sons Cruz, Jesse, and Penn; and my supportive and loving husband, Martin Chourré.

Contents

Map Legend

Interstate	(00)	Campground	▲
US Highway	(00)	Picnic Area	🛆
State or Other Principal Road	(00) (000)	Cabins/Buildings	■
		Peak	9,782 ft.
Forest Road	0000		
		Hill	
Interstate Highway	⟹	Elevation	9,782 ft. ✕
Paved Road	⟹		
		Gate	•—•
Gravel Road	⟹	Mine Site	⚒
Unimproved Road	====▷		
		Overlook/Point of Interest	◘
Trailhead	◯		
Main Trail	--~--		
Secondary Trail	--^--	National Forest/Park Boundary	⌐ ¬ ⌐
Parking Area	Ⓟ	Map Orientation	N
River/Creek	∿		
Marsh	⊻	Scale	0 0.5 1 Miles
One Way Road	One Way ←		

Overview Map – Lake Tahoe

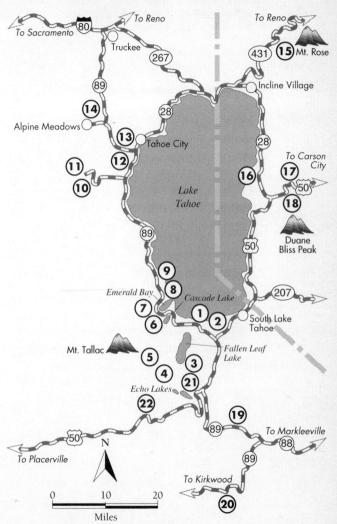

To Sacramento

To Reno

80

Truckee

267

To Reno

431 **15** Mt. Rose

89

14

Alpine Meadows

13 Tahoe City

28

Incline Village

11

12

10

Lake
Tahoe

28

16

To Carson
City

17

50

18

Duane
Bliss Peak

89

50

9

8

Emerald Bay

7

6

Cascade Lake

1 **2**

207

South Lake
Tahoe

Mt. Tallac

5

4

3

Fallen Leaf
Lake

21

Echo Lakes

22

19

To Markleeville

89

88

50

89

To Placerville

N

To Kirkwood

20

0   10   20

Miles

Ranking the Hikes

The following list ranks the hikes in this book from easiest to hardest.

Introduction

What is a "best easy" day hike?

Lake Tahoe is a magnet. Deep water cradled in a sawtoothed bowl of granite peaks high in the Sierra Nevada range, it attracts as only the profound can, with mystery and incomparable beauty.

People are latecomers to the lake's multifaceted wonders. First, there were the Native Americans, who gathered the bounty of summer at the water's edge. Next came the conquerors, first Spaniards and then American fortune hunters, who scoured the high country for mineral wealth. And now come modern travelers, mostly crowding to the lake to enjoy a short holiday, but some choosing to make the scenic heart of the Sierra their home.

This guide to easy hikes is for everyone, whether someone on a short visit, or someone lucky enough to live on Lake Tahoe's shores. These routes are ideal for adventure or contemplation; on a Sunday afternoon with the family or on a summer evening after a hard day's work.

With this book and others like it, Falcon Publishing has allowed me to continue working on a theme generated and brought to fruition when I worked as an author for Chockstone Press. Chockstone's *12 Short Hikes* series described short hikes—generally less than five miles long and two hours in duration—around major metropolitan areas and resort communities. The hikes were selected with the goal of expanding the horizons of visitors, area families, and local folk who were short on time, offering trails of varied length and atmosphere, all charming and all easy.

Easy, of course, is a relative term. Some would argue that no hike in the mountains is easy; nearly all involve a hill climb of some description. To aid in the selection of a hike that suits particular needs and abilities, I've ranked those included herein from easiest to hardest. Bear in mind that even the steepest of these hikes can be made easy by hiking within your limits and taking rests when you need them.

To determine how long it might take you to complete a particular hike, consider that on flat ground, most walkers average two miles per hour. Adjust that rate by the steepness of the terrain and your level of fitness (subtract time if you're an aerobic animal and add time if you're hiking with kids), and you have a ballpark hiking duration. Be sure to add more time if you plan to picnic or take part in other activities like bird watching or photography along the trail.

To walk amid the grandeur of nature, whether along a narrow path that delves deeply into wilderness or on a well-kept paved trail, is, I believe, to renew the soul. A guide to best easy day hikes, like this one, suggests routes to that renewal, and has been compiled with the hope that anyone who embarks on a journey into the wild, regardless of its length, will find the peace and inspiration that I have found there.

— *Tracy Salcedo*

Leave No Trace

Lake Tahoe is a popular place. The trails that weave through its backcountry are heavily used in the summer months, and sometimes take a real beating. Because of their proximity to pollution and dense population we, as trail users and advocates, must be especially vigilant to make sure our passing leaves no lasting mark.

Equate traveling these trails to visiting a museum. You obviously avoid leaving a mark on an art treasure in the museum. If everyone who visited the museum left one tiny mark, the piece of art would be destroyed—and what would a building full of trashed art be worth? The same goes for these trails. If we all left just one little mark on the landscape, the parks and wildlands would soon be despoiled.

These trails can accommodate plenty of human travel if everybody treats them with respect. Just a few thoughtless, badly mannered, or uninformed visitors can ruin them for everyone who follows. The book *Leave No Trace* is a valuable resource for learning more about these principles.

Three Falcon Principles of Leave No Trace

- *Leave with everything you brought with you.*
- *Leave no sign of your visit.*
- *Leave the landscape as you found it.*

Litter is the scourge of all trails. It is unsightly, polluting, and potentially dangerous to wildlife. Pack out all your own trash, including biodegradable items like orange peels, which might be sought out by area critters. You might also pack out garbage left trailside by less considerate hikers.

Don't approach or feed any wild creatures—the ground squirrel eyeing your snack food is best able to survive if it remains self-reliant, since it is not likely to find cookies along the trail when winter comes.

Please, don't pick the wildflowers—or gather rocks, antlers, feathers, and other treasures you see along the trail. Removing these items will only take away from the next hiker's backcountry experience.

Avoid damaging trailside soils and plants by remaining on the established route. Don't cut switchbacks, which can promote erosion. Leaving the trail also may mean trampling fragile vegetation, especially at high altitude. Select durable surfaces, like rocks, logs,, or sandy areas, for resting spots.

Be courteous by not making loud noises while hiking.

Many of these trails are multi-use, which means you'll share them with other hikers, trail runners, mountain bikers, and equestrians. Familiarize yourself with the proper trail etiquette, yielding the trail when appropriate.

If possible, use outhouses at trailheads or along the trail. If not, pack in a lightweight trowel and a plastic bag so that you can bury your waste 6 to 8 inches deep and pack out used toilet paper. Make sure you relieve yourself at least 300 feet away from any surface water or boggy spot.

Remember to abide by the golden rule of backcountry travel: If you pack it in, pack it out!

Leave no trace—put your ear to the ground and listen carefully. Thousands of people coming behind you are thankful for your courtesy and good sense.

Be Prepared

Generally, hiking in the Lake Tahoe basin is good, safe fun, but you must exercise caution as well as your legs. There is much you can do to ensure each outing is safe and enjoyable. I encourage all hikers to verse themselves completely in the science of backcountry travel—it's knowledge worth having and it's easy to acquire.

Some specific advice:

Know the basics of first aid, including how to treat bleeding, bites and stings, and fractures, strains, or sprains. None of these hikes is so remote that help can't be reached within a short time, but you'd be wise to carry and know how to use simple supplies, like over-the-counter pain relievers, bandages, and ointments. Pack a first-aid kit on each excursion.

Familiarize yourself with the symptoms and treatment of altitude sickness (especially if you are visiting the area from a significantly lesser altitude). If you or one of your party exhibits any symptom of this potentially fatal condition, including headache, nausea, or unusual fatigue, seek medical attention.

Know the symptoms of both cold- and heat-related conditions, including hypothermia and heat stroke. The best way to avoid these afflictions is to wear appropriate clothing, drink lots of water, eat enough to keep the internal fires properly stoked, and keep a pace that is within your physical limits.

The sun at these altitudes (all these hikes are above 5,000

feet) can be brutal, so wear a strong sunscreen. Afternoon and evening thunderstorms, while rare, harbor a host of potential hazards, including rain, hail, and lightning. Retreat to the safety of the car or other shelter if you suspect the weather will turn, and carry protective clothing.

Keep children under careful watch. Waterways move deceptively fast, animals and plants may harbor danger, and rocky terrain and cliffs are potential hazards. Children should carry a plastic whistle; if they become lost, they should stay in one place and blow the whistle to summon help.

You'll enjoy each of these hikes much more if you wear good socks and hiking boots. Carry a comfortable backpack loaded with water, snacks, and extra clothing, including a warm hat, gloves, and a jacket, and the appropriate maps. Pack a camera, binoculars, or a good novel to curl up with on a warm rock—or any other item that will heighten your enjoyment of these hikes.

1
TALLAC HISTORIC SITE AND TALLAC POINT

Type of hike: Loop.
Total distance: 2 miles.
Elevation gain: 80 feet.
Maps: USGS Emerald Bay; USDA Forest Service Lake Tahoe Basin Management Unit Map; Tom Harrison Recreation Map of Lake Tahoe.
Starting point: Tallac Historic Site trailhead, Lake Tahoe Visitor Center, South Lake Tahoe.
Finding the trailhead: From the intersection of U.S. Highway 50 and California 89 in South Lake Tahoe, go north on CA 89 for 3.1 miles to the turnoff for the Tallac Historic Site. Turn right onto Heritage Way, and follow it for 0.3 mile to the parking area. Begin on the Historic Estates Trail, which is at the southeast end of the parking area.

Key points:
0.5 Tour the historic sites.
1.0 Hike along the lakeside path.
1.2 Reach Tallac Point.
1.6 Pass the visitor center.

The hike: Lake Tahoe has proven itself the perfect habitat for a variety of inhabitants, from the Washoe Indians who summered on its shores, to the modern vacationers who built

7

Tallac Historic Site, Rainbow Trail

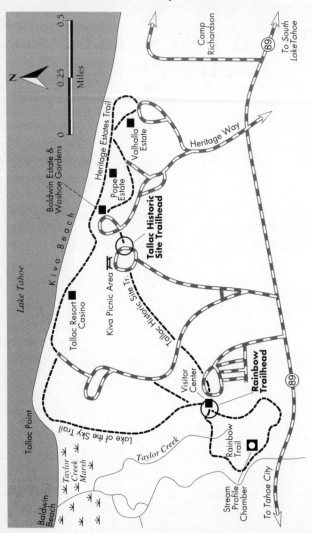

Camp Richardson

89

To South Lake Tahoe

N

0.25 0.5

Miles

0

Heritage Way

Heritage Estates Trail

Valhalla Estate

Baldwin Estate & Washoe Gardens

Pope Estate

Kiva Beach

Tallac Historic Site Trailhead

Lake Tahoe

Kiva Picnic Area

Tallac Historic Site Tr.

Tallac Resort Casino

Rainbow Trailhead

Visitor Center

89

Tallac Point

Lake of the Sky Trail

Rainbow Trail

Taylor Creek Marsh

Taylor Creek

Stream Profile Chamber

To Tahoe City

Baldwin Beach

grand estates, to the myriad of wild creatures—deer, eagles, and trout, to name a few—that have called the lake home for thousands of years. This trail loop offers glimpses of what all these groups have found here and shows the marks they have left on the landscape.

Begin by following the paved path south from the parking area through the Washoe Gardens and the Baldwin Estate. A series of interpretive signs describes the buildings and other historic sites you'll pass as you tour the site; visit the buildings, museums, and gift shops at your leisure.

Beyond the Baldwin enclave lies the Pope Estate; stay to the right (southwest), as you will have a chance to wander through the gardens and arboretum on the return trip. Pass the engine and propeller of the *Tod Goodwin*, the last large wooden steamer to navigate Lake Tahoe. Next comes Valhalla, then the Heller Estate at 0.5 mile, and its Boathouse Theater, which stages theatrical productions.

Loop left at the far end of the Valhalla Estate to pick up the lakeside path, following it back through the Pope garden and arboretum and passing through the gate into the Baldwin Estate. Beyond the Baldwin guest cottages, pass through another gate and take the bark-covered path to the right. The path veers toward the lake at 1.0 mile, then parallels the shore, passing a number of beach access points and picnic sites.

The lakeside trail meanders through the riparian habitat that clings to the lakeshore, passing the foundation of the Tallac Resort Casino. The trail splits just beyond; stay right (adjacent to the lake).

The path curls around Tallac Point, which offers great lake views and an interpretive sign that names the peaks and points at 1.2 miles. Baldwin Beach and the Taylor Creek Marsh lie to your right (northwest) as you continue. At the four-way intersection, take the middle road, following the fence that protects the marsh. At the next intersection, stay right (northwest), and visit the viewing platform overlooking the marsh.

The trail continues past interpretive signs quoting John Muir and Mark Twain. The visitor center lies beyond the amphitheater at 1.6 miles. From this point, bear left (south and across the street) on the Tallac Historic Site Trail, which skirts the parking area. Cross another road and follow the sign for the historic site and Kiva Picnic Area, heading left (northeast) at the trail crossing. Cross another roadway and meander through the gray-green scrubland and open woods to the parking area.

2
RAINBOW TRAIL

Type of hike: Loop.

See map on page 8

Total distance: 1 mile.
Elevation gain: Minimal.
Maps: USGS Emerald Bay; USDA Forest Service Lake Tahoe Basin Management Unit Map; Tom Harrison Recreation Map of Lake Tahoe.
Starting point: Lake Tahoe Visitor Center, South Lake Tahoe.
Finding the trailhead: To reach the Lake Tahoe Visitor Center from the intersection of U.S. Highway 50 and California 89 in South Lake Tahoe, go north on CA 89 for 3.2 miles to the turnoff for the Lake Tahoe Visitor Center. Turn right on the visitor center road, and follow it to the parking area for the visitor center.

Key points:
0.2 Reach the trail fork.
0.5 Visit the stream profile chamber.

The hike: The amber-tinted waters rise to about five feet, and in them, the fearsome kokanee salmon, the scales on his body a vivid lipstick-red, seems to pace in lovesick agitation, anticipating his autumnal rites of passion. He mingles with his drabber cousins: rainbow, brown and Lahontan cutthroat trout, the latter of which is native to the deep waters of Lake Tahoe. The larger fish, some of a size that would make anglers salivate, circle lazily in the clear pool, while the smaller dart about swiftly, looking for food or perhaps hoping to avoid becoming a meal themselves.

The Taylor Creek Stream Profile Chamber offers visitors the chance to observe these creatures in detail, often with the assistance of an interpretive naturalist. The stream aquarium is not the only attraction in the chamber; a well-designed interpretive display imparts a variety of information about the ecology and inhabitants of Lake Tahoe and its environs.

The stream profile chamber lies at about the halfway point on a short, pleasant paved walk that is wheelchair-accessible and easy enough for a toddler to enjoy. The route is lined with interpretive signs and benches, perfect tools to entertain and delight children of all ages.

The path begins just outside the visitor center building, and curves northwest around interpretive signs and through an aspen glen. At the trail fork at 0.2 mile, go right (following the arrow); an interpretive sign describes how national forests act as giant sponges. Meander through the meadow, rife with wildflowers in early summer, then cross the marsh on the boardwalks, which lead along Taylor Creek to a tiny, sunny streamside beach.

From the beach, the trail dives back into the aspen. A couple of bridges span various aspects of the creek; the cool, clear water swirls around the smooth, marble-like rocks that line its bed.

The trail forks at the stream profile chamber at 0.5 mile. Take the left fork down the hill to visit the chamber. Follow the exit sign in the chamber to the path that leads up and onto the Rainbow Trail, and go left, continuing on the loop. Amid the aspen you will pass a "pillow sensor" and rain gauge, and an interpretive display that explains their functions. Beyond lies an alder spring, and then the tall grasses and wildflowers of the meadow lead you back to the trail fork. Go right, and up, to the visitor center and parking area.

Angora Lakes

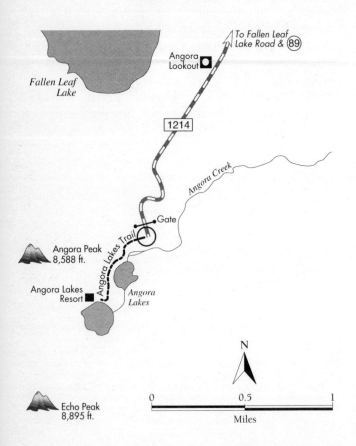

3
ANGORA LAKES

Type of hike: Out-and-back.
Total distance: 1 mile.
Elevation gain: 160 feet.
Maps: USGS Echo Lakes; USDA Forest Service Lake Tahoe Basin Management Unit Map; Tom Harrison Recreation Map of Lake Tahoe.
Starting point: Angora Lakes trailhead, Fallen Leaf Lake.
Finding the trailhead: From the intersection of U.S. Highway 50 and California 89 in South Lake Tahoe, go north on CA 89 for 3 miles to Fallen Leaf Lake Road. Turn left (west) on Fallen Leaf Lake Road and go 2 miles to Tahoe Mountain Road. Turn left (southwest) on Tahoe Mountain Road and follow it for 0.4 mile to Forest Road 1214. Turn right (west) on FR 1214 and travel 3 miles to the trailhead parking area at the end of the road. The trailhead is beyond the gate at the south end of the parking area.

Key points:
0.2 Reach Lower Angora Lake.
0.5 Rest on the shores of Upper Angora Lake.

The hike: Pack your towels and bring the kids: The Angora Lakes trail is short, sweet, and lip-smacking good—the perfect introduction to hiking in the mountains!

After a short romp up a wide, flat trail (with enough elevation gain to get sturdy little hearts pumping), you will land on the sandy shores of Upper Angora Lake, replete with a spectacular alpine setting, cool water for swimming, rowboats for rent, and a snack bar that features some of the best lemonade money can buy. It's definitely not a wilderness experience, but the hike has a lot of charm and offers a brief opportunity to begin an education on the nature of the Sierra Nevada.

Begin by following the wide path as it loops in broad arcing turns up a boulder-strewn, forested hillside. After the short climb, the path flattens and is intersected by social paths that lead right (south) toward private residences on Lower Angora Lake. Stay left (west) on the main track, which tops a rise, then skirts the bucolic wooded shores of Lower Angora Lake at 0.2 mile.

Shortly, signs indicate you're near the Angora Lakes Resort. Another exceptionally brief climb leads to the snack bar and cabins that circle the eastern reaches of Upper Angora Lake. The western shores are contained by black-streaked terraced cliffs that spill down from Echo and Angora peaks. The beach hugs the north shore; stake out a swath of sand, sip some of the luscious lemonade served up at the snack stand, and enjoy.

4
GRASS LAKE

Type of hike: Out-and-back.
Total distance: 5 miles.
Elevation gain: 690 feet.
Maps: USGS Emerald Bay and Echo Lakes; USDA Forest Service Lake Tahoe Basin Management Unit Map; Tom Harrison Recreation Map of Lake Tahoe.
Starting point: Glen Alpine trailhead at Lily Lake.
Finding the trailhead: From the intersection of U.S. Highway 50 and California 89 in South Lake Tahoe, take CA 89 north for 3.0 miles to Fallen Leaf Lake Road. Turn left (west) on Fallen Leaf Lake Road and follow it for 5.0 miles, past the lodge and marina, to a fork. Go left (west) on Forest Road 1216, following the sign for Lily Lake. The trailhead parking area is 0.6 mile ahead, across the bridge. Restrooms are available. The trailhead is at the northwest end of the parking lot, marked by a green metal gate. A wilderness permit is required for day use, and is available at the trailhead.

Key points:
0.4 Pass the waterfall.
1.0 The road narrows to a single track.
1.5 Arrive at trail intersection.
2.4 Reach Grass Lake.

Grass Lake

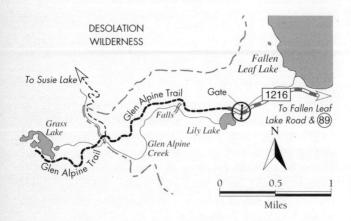

The hike: Water, water everywhere: two lakes, two waterfalls, and three creek crossings … and in early season, or during heavy snow years, the trail itself may even be half submerged in flowing snowmelt. The stretch of the Glen Alpine Trail from Lily Lake to Grass Lake can be a bit soggy, but with the abundance of water, be it burbling, cascading, or still, this is an invigorating hike.

At the outset, the trail is a pebbly access road for cabins located on private land. A short distance up the road, you will pass warning signs and a gate at the entrance to private land. At the fork, go right (northwest) and up, as directed by the sign on the tree.

Patches of asphalt are interspersed with the pebbles as you approach the first series of cascades at 0.4 mile, the largest of which is about 30 feet in height. The display is best (and loudest) in June and July. Past the falls, the trail climbs to another intersection; go left (west), following the trail sign.

The road rambles past private cabins through a lovely mixed evergreen forest with a lush understory of wild berries and flowers. Just beyond an old barn, another trail sign points you to the right (and westward).

At the 1.0 mile point, the road ends at a trail marker, and the singletrack begins. Climb the rustic staircase and watch for lizards sunning themselves on the granite. A switchback leads up and over a granite hummock and continues to climb west.

A trail fork lies just beyond the Desolation Wilderness sign at 1.5 miles. The sign points you left (west) to Grass Lake. The first creek crossing lies just beyond: Cross via the tumble of logs that serves as a bridge, which lies just upstream of the trail proper (in August and September, you may be able to hop rocks across the creek). Once across, go left a short distance to pick up the path, which continues through the forest to a granite slab overlooking the second creek crossing.

Ford the second stream using two logs that span the mouth of the shallow granite gorge. This can be a bit tricky if the water is high—swallow your pride and go on hands and knees if you are more comfortable.

The trail continues west through interwoven woodland and open terrain, winding up to the third creek crossing.

Beyond, a series of short granite and timber staircases lead up the small ramparts of granite that lie below the lake. Travel a final stretch through a brushy gully; you emerge at lakeside at 2.4 miles.

Grass Lake is contained by low, rolling expanses of granite and clusters of fir, pine, and brush. To the west, a spectacular waterfall spills off a red rock cliff; beyond and above the lake and falls, the arcing walls of the high glacial basin rise skyward. These walls are imposing and comforting at the same time, gently cradling the placid lake at the end of the trail. Return as you came.

Options: From the trail intersection at the 1.5-mile mark, you can head right and up to a variety of other alpine lakes, including Susie Lake, and also up the west side of Mount Tallac.

5
MOUNT TALLAC TRAIL TO CATHEDRAL LAKE

Type of hike: Out-and-back.
Total distance: 4.2 miles.
Elevation gain: 1,160 feet.
Maps: USGS Emerald Bay; USDA Forest Service Lake Tahoe Basin Management Unit Map; Tom Harrison Recreation Map of Lake Tahoe.
Starting point: Mount Tallac trailhead.
Finding the trailhead: From the intersection of U.S. Highway 50 and California 89 in South Lake Tahoe, head north on CA 89 for 4.1 miles to the turnoff for Camp Shelly and the Mount Tallac trailhead. Turn left (west) onto the trailhead road, and drive 0.4 mile to the first fork in the road. Go left (southwest), following the arrow for the Tallac trailhead. After 0.2 mile, reach another intersection; stay straight (right) on Forest Road 1306. The trailhead parking area is 0.5 mile ahead. The well-signed trailhead is at the west end of the parking area. A wilderness permit, which is available at the trailhead, is required for day use.

Key points:
0.5 Attain the ridge.
1.5 Reach Floating Island Lake.
2.1 Arrive at Cathedral Lake.

Mount Tallac Trail to Cathedral Lake

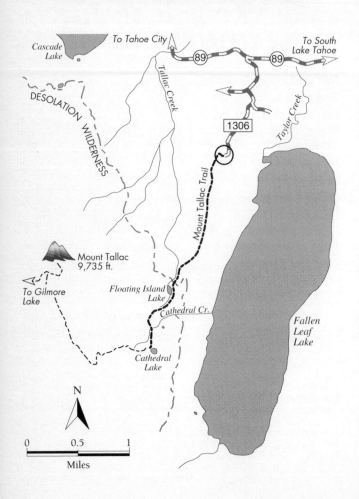

The hike: Statuesque Mount Tallac, which dominates nearly every South Lake Tahoe vista, is an especially powerful presence on this hike. Separated from its gray-green flanks only by a narrow glacial valley for most of the hike, every foot of the trail is shadowed by the daunting but mostly peaceful spirit of Tallac's summit. Cathedral Lake lies at the terminus of one of the mountain's many talus fields; from this peaceful tarn, the trail climbs relentlessly to the top.

The trail begins flat and shady, but that ends shortly, as you climb a steep, hot section through sunny scrubland scented with sage. Ascend a couple of switchbacks, the first of which offers a wonderful view of Fallen Leaf Lake, directly below (south), and Lake Tahoe, behind and east.

At 0.5 mile, the trail reaches the narrow ridgetop of the lateral moraine that separates Fallen Leaf Lake from Mount Tallac. Now a gentle ascent with wonderful views of the mountain and lake, the trail cruises along the spine of the moraine through Jeffrey pine and mountain hemlock.

Drop off the ridge into a drainage; the views are abandoned for shade. The trail rollercoasters through forest and gully as it veers north into the shadow of the mountain. You'll climb up to and then alongside the creek that issues from Floating Island Lake, though the trail will flatten and pull away from the stream before cresting the rise at the shores of the small, green lake. At 1.5 miles, you enter the Desolation Wilderness.

Skirt the forested south shore of Floating Island Lake; beyond, the trail veers right (north) before the small talus field and climbs steeply above it. Cross a small meadow and climb over the fallen log to the creek crossing (stay left on the main trail). Beyond, the trail traverses a hillside that is strewn with colorful wildflowers in early summer. Drop briefly through the woods to a second creek crossing, and meander up the drainage to a trail sign. Turn right (northwest), following the sign to Cathedral Lake. Rest on the shores of the small tarn at 2.1 mile, then return to the trailhead by the same route.

Option: If you've the will and strength, you can make the steep climb to the summit of Mount Tallac (9,735 feet; 2.4 miles beyond Cathedral Lake).

6
WHITE CLOUD FALLS

Type of hike: Out-and-back.
Total distance: 2 miles.
Elevation loss: 80 feet.
Maps: USGS Emerald Bay; USDA Forest Service Lake Tahoe Basin Management Unit Map; Tom Harrison Recreation Map of Lake Tahoe.
Starting point: Bayview trailhead in Bayview Campground.
Finding the trailhead: From the intersection of U.S. Highway 50 and California 89 in South Lake Tahoe, head north on CA 89 for 9.4 miles to a left turn into the Bayview Campground. From Tahoe City, follow CA 89 south for 18.9 miles, past the parking areas for Vikingsholm and Eagle Falls, to a right turn into the campground. Follow the campground road 0.3 mile to the limited parking at the trailhead. Direct access to the trailhead may be difficult in high season; be prepared to park in other public parking areas or in safe parking areas along the highway and hike through the campground to the trailhead.

Key points:
0.5 Traverse above Cascade Lake.
1.0 Reach the White Cloud Falls overlook.

The hike: The quiet ramble through an enveloping evergreen forest is a peaceful preamble to the rocky path and raucous

White Cloud Falls, Eagle Lake, Vikingsholm and Emerald Point

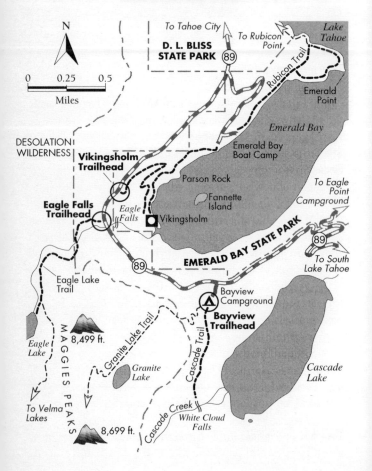

N

0   0.25   0.5
Miles

To Tahoe City

To Rubicon Point

Lake Tahoe

D. L. BLISS STATE PARK

89

Rubicon Trail

Emerald Point

Emerald Bay

Emerald Bay Boat Camp

DESOLATION WILDERNESS

Vikingsholm Trailhead

Parson Rock

Fannette Island

Eagle Falls Trailhead

Eagle Falls

Vikingsholm

To Eagle Point Campground

89

EMERALD BAY STATE PARK

89

To South Lake Tahoe

Eagle Lake Trail

89

Bayview Campground

Bayview Trailhead

8,499 ft.

Granite Lake Trail

Eagle Lake

M A G G I E S   P E A K S

Granite Lake

Cascade Trail

Cascade Lake

To Velma Lakes

8,699 ft.

Cascade Creek

White Cloud Falls

waterfall that lies at the end of this hike. Cascade Creek feeds both the swift falls and Cascade Lake, a dark, still pool that is surrounded by private property and off-limits to hikers. Settle in on the sunny rocks above the cascade and enjoy its cooling mists, along with views of Lake Tahoe.

To begin the hike, walk behind the information kiosk and turn left on Cascade Trail. Climb through the mixed evergreen forest. The trail bends around two short trail posts. Climb a short, rustic stairway to overlook the falls, Cascade Lake, and Lake Tahoe.

At about the half-mile mark, the trail begins a rocky downward traverse of the slope above Cascade Lake. After walking amid low-growing scrub, pick your way through rocks to the base of a black granite cliff. Take care here, as the footing is uneven.

Cross a relatively narrow ledge, then climb granite steps and slabs. Reach an area of talus; a rock cairn (a stack of rocks used as a trail marker, sometimes called a "duck") sits on a nearby boulder. Stay right (west) through the talus field, following a short sequence of cairns. The trail narrows into a drainage. Veer left (south) at the cairn and follow the route down. Make another sharp left, curving back east toward Cascade Lake, then follow the rock-lined path as it crosses a big slab. A flat grassy area lies to the right; Cascade Creek and its spectacular falls lie at the edge of the slab at 1.0 mile. Return as you came.

Option: Bayview Campground also serves as the trailhead for Granite Lake, which lies 1.0 mile from the trailhead. A wilderness permit for day use is required.

7
EAGLE LAKE

See map on page 26

Type of hike: Out-and-back.
Total distance: 2 miles.
Elevation gain: 400 feet.
Maps: USGS Emerald Bay; USDA Forest Service Lake Tahoe Basin Management Unit Map; Tom Harrison's Recreation Map of Lake Tahoe.
Starting point: Eagle Falls trailhead at Eagle Falls Picnic Area.
Finding the trailhead: From the intersection of U.S. Highway 50 and California 89 in South Lake Tahoe, head north on CA 89 for 10.3 miles to the Eagle Falls parking area. From Tahoe City, follow CA 89 south for 18 miles, past the parking area for Vikingsholm, to the Eagle Falls parking area on the right. Parking may be a problem in high season; there is a small fee to park in the lot and limited parking is available along the road. Please be courteous and safe in selecting a parking space. The Eagle Falls trailhead lies beyond the picnic area and restrooms at the parking area. A wilderness permit is required and is available at the trailhead.

Key points:
0.2 Cross the bridge over the falls.
0.9 Arrive at the trail intersection.
1.0 Reach Eagle Lake.

The hike: The bare, cathedral-like walls of a stark Desolation Wilderness canyon form the backdrop for Eagle Lake. You will traverse above a narrow drainage on a well-worn path, with the jagged crowns of the canyon's walls rising on either side of the creek. Dark and clear, Eagle Lake sits in a basin bordered by talus slopes and great black-streaked cliffs. A small island sits slightly off-center in the midst of the calm lake, isolated by frigid mountain water.

Before you hit the trail, fill out a wilderness permit. Begin on stairs that lead up the rock-bordered path. As the trail flattens, enjoy views of the falls and the towering pinnacles and great gray domes of the Desolation Wilderness. A twisting stairway leads up, then down, to the vista point and the sturdy bridge that spans the cataract. Cross the bridge at 0.2 mile and climb the rocky trail past the wilderness boundary signs and up to a large, flat slab dotted with pine and cedar. Skirt another slab and veer left through a colonnade of standing silver snags.

The trail skirts a rock outcrop overlooking the lush creekbed below, then meanders through the forest. Gentle climbing takes you to a trail junction at 0.9 mile, from which you can head deeper into the Desolation Wilderness. To reach Eagle Lake, however, you'll want to bear right (west) toward the giant cirque, following the arrow on the sign.

Scramble down to the shores of Eagle Lake at 1.0 mile. A sprinkling of cedar, ponderosa, and Jeffrey pine provide shade from the vivid alpine sunshine. If you don't mind icy water, Eagle Lake invites a dip. There is no beach, however, so you'll have to dry off and/or enjoy the stunning views from a perch on a tree stump or a sunbaked granite slab.

Return as you came, pausing to enjoy the views of Lake Tahoe on the descent.

Options: From the trail intersection just before Eagle Lake, you can head into the far reaches of the Desolation Wilderness. The next nearest destination is the Velma Lakes (5.0 miles from the Eagle Falls trailhead); beyond lies a web of trails offering an abundance of hiking and backpacking possibilities.

8
VIKINGSHOLM AND EMERALD POINT

Type of hike: Out-and-back.

See map on page 26

Total distance: 5 miles.

Elevation loss: 410 feet.

Maps: USGS Emerald Bay; USDA Forest Service Lake Tahoe Basin Management Unit Map; Tom Harrison Recreation Map of Lake Tahoe.

Starting point: Vikingsholm trailhead at Emerald Bay State Park.

Finding the trailhead: To reach Emerald Bay State Park from the intersection of U.S. Highway 50 and California 89 in South Lake Tahoe, head north on CA 89 for 10.7 miles to the large Emerald Bay State Park parking area on the right (southeast). From Tahoe City, take CA 89 south for 17.6 miles (parking is on the left). If there is no space available here, you will have to park at Eagle Falls or in safe areas along the road. The trail begins on the east end of the parking area, to the left of the huge rock slab.

Key points:

0.5 Reach Vikingsholm.

1.8 Pass Parsons Rock.

2.5 Reach Emerald Point.

The hike: A summertime trip to Lake Tahoe wouldn't be complete without a visit to Emerald Bay. Ocean-green and opalescent, it's quite obvious how this gleaming arm of Tahoe earned its name. Not so obvious is the jewel of a trail that leads along the shore of the bay to its narrow mouth and beyond. This trail doesn't see the traffic that spills down the road to the storied Vikingsholm estate; most visitors are content to visit the house, which can be toured, and picnic on the white sand beach in its front yard. The more adventurous will find lovely views and relative solitude on the flat, forested path to Emerald Point. Walk quietly and watchfully as you near the point; you may see an eagle or osprey that has returned to a lakeside roost after years of absence.

Begin by heading down the wide path (a human highway in the busy summer season). Go around two switchbacks to a trail intersection with a park map. Take the right-hand trail downhill, through the open woodland, to the cluster of buildings that make up Vikingsholm. Follow the trail to the front of the old home at 0.5 mile.

To pick up the Rubicon Trail, which leads out to Emerald Point, loop back left (north) toward the Vikingsholm Trail along the bayshore, following the sandy path past the dock and swim beach. Go left (northwest) to the trail intersection for Emerald Point, then turn right (east) onto the trail proper. Pass through the picnic area to a bridge crossing the narrow creek.

The trail continues at bayside, wandering through the woods that line the shore and passing a side trail that leads right (south) to a rock outcrop. Cross a drainage littered with rock and deadfall, being careful to stay on the trail. Be cautious if there is high water in the gully (during early season)—a bridge farther up the hillside offers safe passage.

Pass Parsons Rock at 1.8 miles; the bayside views make this a good choice for a break. The trail leads into the Emerald Bay Boat Camp, merging with the camp road. Beyond the campground, the road splits. Go right (east) on the Rubicon Trail, passing the No Dogs sign.

At the Emerald Point Bypass sign, stay right (east) to Emerald Point. The route passes through a marsh to the narrow beach at the point (2.5 miles). This last section of trail may be closed for raptor nesting. Return as you came.

Option: If you take the Emerald Bay Bypass, you will continue north on the Rubicon Trail through the lovely shorelands preserved within neighboring D. L. Bliss State Park to Rubicon Point (4.5 miles one-way from Vikingsholm).

The Lighthouse and Rubicon Point

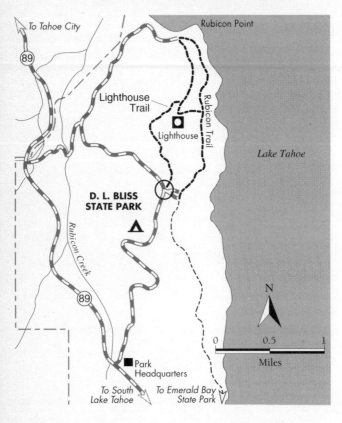

9
THE LIGHTHOUSE AND RUBICON POINT

Type of hike: Loop.
Total distance: 2.5 miles.
Elevation gain/loss: +200/-400 feet.
Maps: USGS Emerald Bay; USDA Forest Service Lake Tahoe Basin Management Unit Map; Tom Harrison Recreation Map of Lake Tahoe.
Starting point: Lighthouse trailhead at D. L. Bliss State Park.
Finding the trailhead: To reach D. L. Bliss State Park and the trailhead from the intersection of U.S. Highway 50 and California 89 in South Lake Tahoe, head north on CA 89 for 12.5 miles to the turnoff for D. L. Bliss State Park, which is on the east side of the highway. From Tahoe City, take CA 89 south for 15.8 miles to the park entrance. Follow the park road 1.0 mile east to the trailhead, which is on the left side of the road (park in the small lot across the street). A limited number of visitors are admitted to the park; if you arrive after 10 A.M., check at the visitor center for availability. There is a fee.

Key points:
0.8 Visit the lighthouse.
1.5 Circle Rubicon Point.
2.4 Reach the final trail intersection.

The hike: The lighthouse that once warned sailors of the watery dangers lurking off Rubicon Point is startlingly small and unassuming. In the early days of the twentieth century, the light within was brilliant with burning acetylene. Now, only sunlight sifted through cracks in the weathered wooden siding illuminates the tiny interior of the structure.

One day in the near future, however, the light may burn again. Plans call for the lighthouse to be rebuilt within the next couple of years, with a new trail leading to it.

The lighthouse isn't the only example of Lake Tahoe's ruggedness found on this route. Farther along, the trail skims a rock wall high above the lake. Views from this aerie are superlative. A word of caution: though protected by a railing, this stretch is not for those afraid of heights or leery of exposure, and children should be watched carefully.

The Lighthouse Trail begins by climbing around a switchback and skirting a fire-scarred section of woodland. The trail flattens amid evergreens and boulders, then drops to a switchback and into a cluster of blackened trees.

Descend through a hauntingly beautiful burned woodland. The lack of canopy allows views of Rubicon Bay and beyond. A corridor of mingled live and dead trees leads down to a trail intersection. Go right (east), then quickly left, under a tree and steeply down. The lighthouse is perched on a rocky shelf at 0.8 mile.

Climb back to the trail crossing and go right on the main trail, switching back and down toward the paved parking area. At the trail junction at the edge of the lot, a footpath leads right (southeast) to the Rubicon Trail. Follow the Rubicon around the point at 1.5 mile.

At the next trail fork, marked with a log, stay right, gently climbing. The trail is spectacularly exposed here; a chain guards the abrupt drop, and head-thumping overhangs loom over the trail. Climb a steep rock staircase and pass a signpost for the lighthouse. Stay left (south) on the Rubicon Trail, enjoying the heavenly views as the trail flattens and traverses the steep hillside above the lake. Watch for osprey, which have been sighted along the trail.

Eventually, the path curves away from the lake into dense forest. At about 2.4 miles, you'll enter a clearing marked with a row of rocks; take the trail to the right (northwest). The dark, needle-carpeted path leads through the trees to the park access road. Go right to return to the trailhead and parking area.

Options: To reach Emerald Point, continue on the Rubicon Trail by staying left at the last intersection noted above; continue around to Vikingsholm if you desire (see Hike 8).

Ellis Lake,
Pacific Crest Trail at Barker Pass

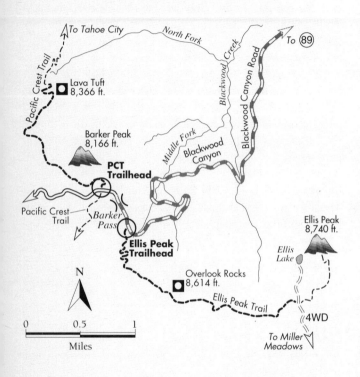

10
ELLIS LAKE

Type of hike: Out-and-back.
Total distance: 5 miles.
Elevation gain: 814 feet.
Maps: USGS Homewood; USDA Forest Service Lake Tahoe Basin Management Unit Map; Tom Harrison Recreation Map of Lake Tahoe.
Starting point: Ellis Peak Trail at Barker Pass.
Finding the trailhead: To reach the Ellis Peak Trail at the summit of Barker Pass from Tahoe City, take California 89 south for 4.4 miles to the turnoff marked Kaspian and Blackwood Canyon. Turn right (west) on Blackwood Canyon Road, and go 7.2 miles to the trailhead, which is on the left (west) side of the road just before the end of the pavement.

Key points:
1.2 Climb onto the overlook rocks.
2.2 Reach the trail intersection.
2.5 Arrive at Ellis Lake.

The hike: The splendor of the northern Sierra is powerfully vivid when viewed from a perch atop the rocky ridge crested by the Ellis Peak Trail. Cliffs drop sharply into the green valley of Blackwood Canyon, with Lake Tahoe a vast inky stain on the gray and green landscape. To the west lie the forbidding, gunmetal gray ramparts of the Desolation Wilderness, an impressive landscape of flowing granite, lingering snowfields, and small, iridescent lakes.

Beyond this aerie, the Sierra shows yet another aspect of its makeup. Towering firs create a shady canopy overhead, and needles dense on the forest floor quiet the footfalls of hikers. The thunderhead-dark battlements of Ellis Peak rise above peaceful Ellis Lake, a pretty tarn in a classic alpine setting of evergreens and talus.

This hike begins with a relatively brutal climb, but it is eminently rewarding. Head up out of the parking lot to the left (southeast), passing a trail sign. Steep, *steep* switchbacks lead onto the ridge. The views begin as you enter a field dense with broad-leafed mule ear. Tortured evergreens turn barren backsides to the prevailing west wind, forming a lonely windbreak as the route dips in and out of rocky saddles. Outcrops of crumbling stone hover over Blackwood Canyon, offering stunning viewpoints of Lake Tahoe and the High Sierra.

The top of the last small summit basks in uninterrupted sunlight, tundra grasses, and warm summer winds. Wind-lashed trees hook over the path; look for a short side trail leading left (east) onto a lovely rock perch at 1.2 miles. From this overlook, 360-degree views can be enjoyed.

Beyond the overlook rocks, the trail begins to descend into the forest. The drop begins gradually, but steepens as the woodland grows denser, steeper and deeper until the angle moderates amid thick, lichen-coated firs.

Skirt a meadow on the right (west) side of the trail, then

begin a gentle climb. The trail follows banking curves through a magnificent stand of old firs, traversing upward to a marked junction where the trail intersects a rough gravel road at 2.2 miles. Go left (east) on the roadway, passing a shallow pond that lies in a depression on the left (north) side of the road.

Drop a short distance on the road, circling around a talus field that spills from the cliffs of Ellis Peak, to bottle-green Ellis Lake at 2.5 miles. Willows guard the northern shore, with a slope covered in soft forest litter climbing gently to the trail. A mixed fir forest with an open canopy circles three-quarters of the lake, but on the south shore a steep spill of talus pours into the water, and alpine scrub hugs the slope above the rockfall. Once you've enjoyed the lake's amenities, even taking a swim if the weather permits, return as you came.

Options: The trail intersection above the lake offers a couple of choices if you wish to extend your hike. The singletrack that rises straight ahead (south) climbs to Ellis Peak. The road to the right (west) eventually drops to the McKinney Rubicon Trail near Miller Meadows and Miller Lake.

11
PACIFIC CREST TRAIL AT BARKER PASS

See map on page 38

Type of hike: Out-and-back.
Total distance: 3 miles.
Elevation gain: 660 feet.
Maps: USGS Homewood; USDA Forest Service Lake Tahoe Basin Management Unit Map; Tom Harrison Recreation Map of Lake Tahoe.
Starting point: Pacific Crest trailhead at Barker Pass.
Finding the trailhead: To reach the trailhead near Barker Pass from Tahoe City, take California 89 for 4.4 miles south to the turnoff marked Kaspian and Blackwood Canyon. Turn right on Blackwood Canyon Road, and go 7.7 miles to the trailhead, which is on the right (east) side of the road beyond both the pass and the end of the pavement.

Key points:
1.0 Check the views from the overlook.
1.5 Arrive at the lava tuft.

The hike: The Pacific Crest Trail (PCT) is a wilderness enthusiast's dream. Riding the high ground from the snowy northern reaches of Washington south to the deserts of California, this famous trail, like its brethren, the Continental Divide Trail and the Appalachian Trail, provides ample ground for hikers to see America as few ever can.

This short hike offers a sampling of the rigors and beauty of the PCT. It is rugged but well maintained, user-friendly but not overcrowded, and offers wonderful views. At the end of this recommended route, a plug of dark volcanic rock juts from rose-colored earth that slides away into Blackwood Canyon. It is a stark and exposed landscape, mellowed only by the puffy pink blooms of pussy paws that cling to the inhospitable soils.

Begin to the left of the information sign at the parking lot and trailhead, avoiding the more obvious path to the right. Stay left in the trees, which thin into a more open scrubland that offers views south and west into the Desolation Wilderness.

Back in the woods again, you will cross a rocky gully; the trees part as the route traverses another gully stripped bare by winter's avalanches. Pass the national forest boundary sign and continue through lichen-dressed firs into a huge meadow thick with mule ear. The paddle-like leaves rattle in the ever-present breeze. Traverse back into the trees and cross a rugged roadway, continuing on the obvious trail. Logs mark a leftward bend in the path, but a quick right leads to a lovely vista point overlooking Lake Tahoe at 1.0 mile.

To continue, head back into the woods on the main trail. Climb around a switchback, and cross raised footbridges over a verdant stream that nourishes wonderful wildflowers into the dry days of August.

Cross a spectacular avalanche slide path littered with deadwood before you climb through a final stretch of woodland onto an open, barren slope. The trail traverses this exposed area—it looks precarious, but the footing is great. At the saddle at 1.5 miles, the PCT goes left. Take the narrow, unmarked path on the right to the base of the volcanic tuft, and enjoy the views. Don't climb on the lichen-stained rock, as it is not stable. And, unless you have the time and inclination to take on more of the PCT, return via the same route.

Options: The PCT offers options galore; you can explore the reaches of the trail just beyond the end of this description, or you can hike to Mount Rainier in Washington State! This section of the PCT is also part of the Tahoe Rim Trail, which means you also can use it to make a circuit of the high country that rims Lake Tahoe.

12
TRUCKEE RIVER TRAIL

Type of hike: Out-and-back.
Total distance: 8 miles.
Elevation loss: 30 feet.
Maps: USGS Tahoe City; USDA Forest Service Lake Tahoe Basin Management Unit Map; Tom Harrison Recreation Map of Lake Tahoe.
Starting point: Truckee River trailhead in Tahoe City.
Finding the trailhead: To reach this stretch of the Tahoe Rim Trail from the intersection of California Highways 89 and 28 in Tahoe City, go 0.2 mile south on CA 89 to a signed right turn into the trailhead parking area.

Key point:
4.0 Reach Alpine Meadows Road and River Ranch.

The hike: This is one of the easiest and thus one of the most popular trails in north Lake Tahoe. The well-maintained paved surface traces the spectacular Truckee River from Tahoe City to the inn at River Ranch, at the gateway to the Alpine Meadows area. Along the way, you will enjoy views of the sparkling waters of the river, the lush riparian habitat that lines its shores, and the thick forest that climbs from its banks.

For most of the summer, the Truckee River swirls with the revelry of river rafters. You may be charmed and dazzled by the vivid blues and yellows of the rafts, and the spectacular colors of the water wear of the boaters. This riotous rainbow spills onto the trail, where the neon Lycra of cyclists mingles with cooler shades worn by in-line skaters and the pastels worn by babies in strollers.

It is virtually impossible to get lost on this trail; if you wander into the river, or if you find you are sharing pavement with automobiles speeding toward Lake Tahoe, you've strayed from the route. A vivid yellow line down the center of the trail separates downstream traffic from those headed upstream. Proximity to the highway precludes any illusion of this being a wilderness hike, but it makes the perfect family outing, and it is wheelchair accessible.

The trail begins riverside, crosses over the arcing bridge to the north shore of the river, then runs between the broad watercourse and the roadway. Turn left (west) beyond the bridge, and head downstream.

At the trail's outset, you'll pass several businesses and cross a couple of driveways, then drop waterside, where dense willow sometimes hides the meandering river. As you head west, you will cross the driveways of lucky souls whose homes are perched on the riverbanks.

Sandbars in the river offer respite for the rafters; for hikers and other trail users, narrow social paths lead to small rocky and/or sandy beaches that serve as wonderful viewpoints, picnic spots or rest and turnaround spots. Head back whenever you'd like; if you have the time and energy, hike all the way to Alpine Meadows Road and River Ranch at 4 miles. Return as you came.

Truckee River Trail

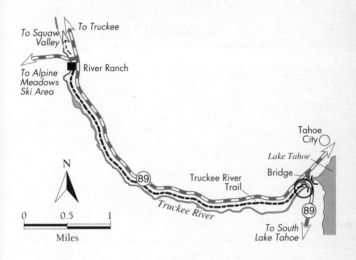

Options: The Truckee River trailhead in Tahoe City also serves as the starting point if you'd like to head in other directions along the paved path, which heads north through and beyond Tahoe City and south toward Homewood.

In addition, the trail is being extended beyond Alpine Meadows Road toward Squaw Valley. If you've the time and inclination, walk farther downriver along the Truckee, enjoying more spectacular riverside scenery.

13
TAHOE RIM TRAIL
AT TAHOE CITY

Type of hike: Out-and-back.
Total distance: 4 miles.
Elevation gain: 880 feet.
Maps: USGS Tahoe City; Tom Harrison Recreation Map of Lake Tahoe.
Starting point: Fairway trailhead in Tahoe City.
Finding the trailhead: To reach this stretch of the Tahoe Rim Trail from the intersection of California Highways 89 and 28 in Tahoe City, take CA 89 west toward Truckee for 0.1 mile. Turn right on Fairway Drive, and go 0.2 mile to the parking lot at the Fairway Community Center. The trailhead is on the left side of the road, opposite the parking lot.

Key points:
0.8 Cross the dirt roadway.
2.0 Reach the vista point.

The hike: So, you're staying in Tahoe City, you want to stretch your legs with a good hike, and you're not into hassling with the traffic that clogs the lakeshore highways. Or, you're looking for a route less traveled, a trail that doesn't see great crowds because it's a bit obscure—the summertime version of the locals' secret powder-filled ski run. You want lake views, you want ferns and big cedar, and you want privacy.

Tahoe Rim Trail at Tahoe City

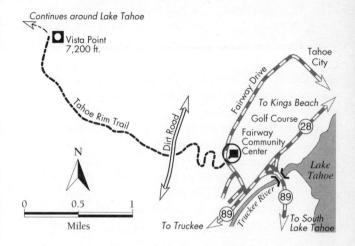

Then take in Tahoe City's section of the Tahoe Rim Trail (TRT), which is located within walking distance of downtown restaurants, and happy host to anyone wishing to wander on the wilder side of Tahoe's laid-back version of urban life.

The TRT, a work in progress as of 1998, will eventually include 150 miles of hiking surface, encircling Lake Tahoe and offering great vistas, delightful hikes of any distance, and access to the Pacific Crest Trail and wilderness areas surrounding the lake.

To begin on the TRT, head uphill past the trail markers, climbing switchbacks through mountain scrub. The trail passes granite outcrops into a woodland with an open canopy that allows sunlight to saturate the lush undergrowth and ripen the sweet berries that thrive on the forest floor.

Keep climbing on the rocky trail, which eventually moves away from the lake and crosses a rocky wilderness access road at 0.8 mile. A white USDA Forest Service post marks the way. Beyond, the forest is punctuated by cedar trees, their north sides bearing the green velvet of lichen.

As you continue through the woods, follow the route across an earthen footbridge and along the relatively flat, meandering path to what appears to be an unused roadway. The small, blue and white plaques that serve as TRT symbols are tacked on the trees, marking the way.

Eventually, the trail switches back through a strip of land bordered on one side by forest and on the other by an open, rocky area. At another switchback, the lake peeks through the trees. The vista point lies above the switchbacks at 2.0 miles, where the dusting of trees lining trail's edge part and the expanse of the inky blue lake becomes visible. This is the spot to turn around, unless you've the time and energy to explore more of the rim trail. Otherwise, retrace your steps back to the Fairway trailhead.

14
FIVE LAKES TRAIL

Type of hike: Out-and-back.
Total distance: 5 miles.
Elevation gain: 1,000 feet.
Maps: USGS Tahoe City and Granite Chief; USDA Forest Service Lake Tahoe Basin Management Unit Map.
Starting point: Granite Chief Wilderness trailhead on Alpine Meadows Road.
Finding the trailhead: To reach the trailhead from the intersection of California Highways 89 and 28 in Tahoe City, follow CA 89 west for 3.6 miles toward Truckee. Turn left on Alpine Meadows Road and go 2.2 miles southwest, toward the ski area, to the trailhead, which lies opposite the second intersection with Deer Park Drive. Park along the main road; the trailhead is just off the pavement adjacent to a Granite Chief Wilderness sign.

Key points:
1.5 Pass the mileage marker and begin the canyon traverse.
2.5 Reach the shores of Five Lakes.

The hike: Three distinct settings, and thus three distinct moods, lie along the trail to Five Lakes. The most arduous part of the climb is at the outset, in a sun-fed thicket of manzanita, mule ear, and snowberry that crowds the steep

Five Lakes Trail

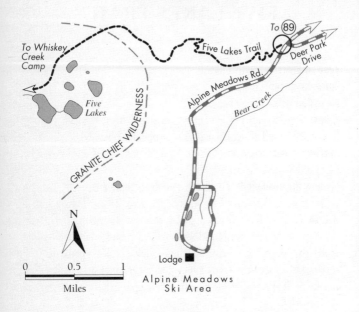

traversing route. Above, grand Jeffrey pines are limited to widely scattered patches of thin soil on the smooth, colorful granite slabs that are a hallmark of the Sierra. Beyond the narrow canyon at the apex of the trail, a thick fir forest takes over, obscuring views and hiding the five small lakes that nestle within its confines. As for the moods—well, the first pitch is vexing; the second section, amid the great rock faces, is thrilling; and the third is shady, peaceful, and contemplative. Enjoy!

Begin by climbing up and left from the trailhead, crossing a series of small drainages as the trail traverses the hillside. Climb switchbacks that cut the slopes below a rampart of rugged ridges.

Switchbacks, switchbacks, and more switchbacks—keep climbing until you leave the scrub behind at a lovely viewpoint. Just beyond, the roots of a huge Jeffrey pine grip a flat spot on the granite. Pass through a small wash; here the trail becomes more exposed and very alpine in feel. Traverse to a switchback, then climb into a saddle.

From the saddle, the trail skirts the edge of a canyon with black-streaked walls. At mile 1.5 a sign notes that Five Lakes lies 1.0 mile ahead. Two switchbacks loop through a tangle of black and orange rock; beyond the jumbled rocks, the trail traverses above the shallowing canyon to more switchbacks. At the outskirts of the fir forest, a sign denotes the boundary of the Granite Chief Wilderness.

Trails collide in the woods: a footpath to the left leads to a lake barely visible through the trees. Stay right on the main path to the second trail fork, and go left to the end of the Five Lakes Trail at 2.5 miles; the path terminates on the shore of one of the small lakes. Unmarked social trails lead to inviting rest spots around the lakes. Visit for a time, then return as you came.

Option: The trail continues to Whiskey Creek Camp and other lovely spots in the Granite Chief Wilderness.

15
TAHOE MEADOWS WHOLE ACCESS TRAIL

Type of hike: Loop.
Total distance: 1.3 miles.
Elevation gain: 40 feet.
Maps: USGS Mount Rose; USDA Forest Service Lake Tahoe Basin Management Unit Map; Tom Harrison Recreation Map of Lake Tahoe.
Starting point: Tahoe Meadows trailhead off Nevada 431.
Finding the trailhead: To reach the trailhead, go north on California 28 from Tahoe City for 14 miles, crossing the Nevada state line and circling the lake to the southern edge of Incline Village. Turn left on Nevada 431. Follow NV 431 for 7.7 miles to a large pullout on the right side of the road. The visitor center and parking area lie just down the slope. Park in the lot if space allows; otherwise, park alongside the road and hike the short distance down to the trailhead.

Key point:
0.7 Reach the head of the meadow.

The hike: It's tough to find an alpine hike that is as flat and friendly as the Tahoe Meadows Whole Access Trail. This easy, scenic route is accessible to the hardy wheelchair user, a family with a small child who won't be restrained by stroller or backpack, or anyone with a hankering for ease and beauty.

Tahoe Meadows Whole Access Trail

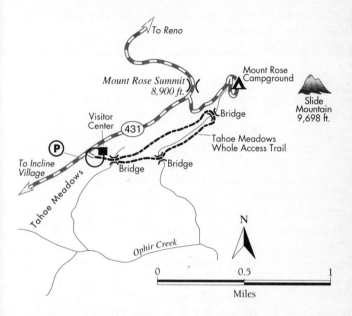

The loop skirts a narrow mountain meadow, offering access to stands of stately evergreens, a chance to sunbathe on a granite slab, and vistas of slopes rich with wildflowers that stretch south to Lake Tahoe and in every other direction to the stony summits of Slide Mountain and her sisters.

A trail sign behind the visitor center marks the hike's start. Go left on the rock-lined path. Almost immediately, enter the meadow and merge with another path. Cross the bridge, then go right, following the blue arrow, across the boardwalk. Go left at the next arrow. To your right (east), a broad expanse of semisterile ground extends upward beyond a bank of evergreens.

The meticulously groomed trail continues across small bridges. At the trail fork, take a short side trip right onto a smooth mound of granite that offers great views of the meadow. Return to the trail, turning right to continue the loop. Leave the trees behind as the trail circumnavigates the meadow.

Cross a boardwalk and go right at the arrow, around a hummock of granite. The next arrow points right, across the bridge. You'll go right again before finally heading left at the next arrow, across another boardwalk.

A series of short bridges leads around the head of the meadow at 0.7 mile, crossing a vigorous stream that feeds the highland marsh. As the trail loops back south and drops ever so gently along the western edge of the meadow, toward the trailhead, you will pass through a stunted forest. Patches of pavement show through the dirt as the trail descends back to the intersection at the first bridge. From here, it's a gentle climb back to the trailhead.

16
SKUNK HARBOR

Type of hike: Out-and-back.
Total distance: 3 miles.
Elevation loss: 570 feet.
Maps: USGS Marlette Lake; USDA Forest Service Lake Tahoe Basin Management Unit Map; Tom Harrison Recreation Map of Lake Tahoe.
Starting point: Skunk Harbor trailhead off Nevada 28.
Finding the trailhead: To reach the trailhead from Tahoe City, go north on California 28, which becomes Nevada 28, for 23.3 miles, passing Incline Village and more developed beaches. There is no sign for the trailhead, which lies just beyond the crest of a forested rise in the highway. The trail is blocked by a green gate tucked below the right (west) side of the road. Park in the narrow pullout alongside the highway above the gate.

From the intersection of U.S. Highway 50 and California 89 in South Lake Tahoe, drive 17.9 miles north on US 50, across the state line, to the intersection of NV 28 at the base of Spooner Summit. Go left (north) onto NV 28, and drive 2.4 miles to the pullout, which is on the left side of the highway.

Caution: The trailhead is not clearly marked, and there is not much parking, which means the route may be difficult to find but also that it will not be crowded.

Key points:
0.6 Arrive at the trail fork before the descent.
1.5 Reach Skunk Harbor.

The hike: Skunk Harbor is no stinker. A broad steep track leads down to this secluded bay, where the clear water of Lake Tahoe washes in a rainbow arc onto the stone-strewn beach, melting from indigo to turquoise to gold as it approaches the shore. This is the site of the Newhall House, built in 1923 as a wedding gift from George Newhall to his wife, Caroline. A plaque explains the origin and preservation of the house, but the true monument is the structure itself. Peek through the windows at the gray interior, and picnic on one of the verandahs, enjoying the wonderful views.

To begin the hike, pass the gate and head down on the pavement, which quickly turns to dirt. The old roadway flattens and circles through a drainage, then traverses the mountainside. From the traverse, you can catch views of Slaughterhouse Canyon and the lake beyond.

When you reach the trail fork at 0.6 mile, stay right (straight) on the broad road. The route drops more steeply, rounding a switchback and passing through a clearing.

Another switchback loops through the thinned woodland; deadwood litters the forest floor where the forest has been cleared and the slash stacked in heaps. Leave the slash zone behind as the trail narrows and enters a swampy area.

Just beyond the moist patch, the trail forks. Go left at the switchback, and meander down through the lush undergrowth, crossing a streamlet, to the Newhall House. Foot-

Skunk Harbor

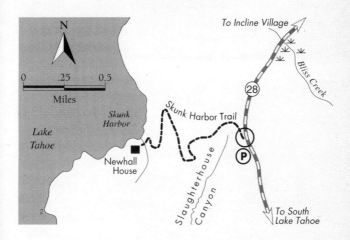

paths lead around to the lake side of the house and Skunk Harbor at 1.5 miles. Explore the rocky beaches, which host the foundations of ruined outbuildings.

Return as you came, keeping in mind that it's all uphill from the bay. It takes a bit longer to climb out than it does to descend.

Option: If you take the trail that departs from the intersection 0.6 mile from the trailhead, above Skunk Harbor, you can descend south into Slaughterhouse Canyon.

Tahoe Rim Trail North and South from Spooner Summit

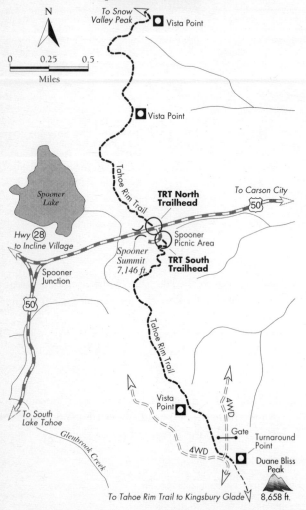

N

0   0.25   0.5
Miles

To Snow Valley Peak   ■ **D** Vista Point

■ **D** Vista Point

Tahoe Rim Trail

TRT North Trailhead   *To Carson City*

Hwy ㉘ to Incline Village

Spooner Lake

Spooner Picnic Area

Spooner Summit 7,146 ft.   **TRT South Trailhead**

Spooner Junction

50

Tahoe Rim Trail

To South Lake Tahoe

Glenbrook Creek

Vista Point

4WD

Gate

Turnaround Point

4WD

To Tahoe Rim Trail to Kingsbury Glade

Duane Bliss Peak 8,658 ft.

17
TAHOE RIM TRAIL NORTH
FROM SPOONER SUMMIT

Type of hike: Out-and-back.
Total distance: 4 miles.
Elevation gain: 440 feet.
Maps: USGS Glenbrook; USDA Forest Service Lake Tahoe Basin Management Unit Map; Tom Harrison Recreation Map of Lake Tahoe.
Starting point: Spooner Summit trailhead off U.S. Highway 50.
Finding the trailhead: To reach the trailhead from Tahoe City, go north on California 28, which becomes Nevada 28, for 25 miles to the intersection of NV 28 and U.S. Highway 50. Turn left on US 50, and go 0.7 miles to Spooner Summit. Turn left into the parking lot, which is on the north side of the highway.

From the intersection of US 50 and California 89 in South Lake Tahoe, drive north on US 50 for 18 miles to the US 50/NV 28 intersection at the base of Spooner Summit. Follow US 50 an additional 0.7 mile to the summit and trailhead.

Key points:
1.2 Reach the first overlook.
2.0 Arrive at the second overlook.

The hike: The trail at Spooner Summit is yet another link in the spectacular Tahoe Rim Trail. The Tahoe Rim Trail leads either way from the summit. The route described for this hike heads north to two overlooks with views of the Carson Valley, a panorama sublime in dusky and sienna hues.

The environmental contrast between the Tahoe basin and the first valley of the Great Basin, which is highlighted along the trail, is thought-provoking. On one side of the divide lies the largest expanse of water in the Sierra Nevada; on the other is a high desert that rolls for a thousand miles to the Rocky Mountains. The juxtaposition is fantastic and inspiring.

The trail is well maintained, straightforward and shady, featuring a steady gentle incline punctuated by the occasional steep section. Hikers can turn around at either overlook, or continue on to Snow Valley Peak and beyond.

To begin, pass the information kiosk and trail signs, staying on the wide main trail. The path traverses through forest and jumbled rock formations. Spooner Lake can be seen through the trees. Cross a willowy drainage, hook right (east), and climb through the open trees.

The path loops through a second broad swale; ignore side trails as you circle onto the opposite slope. The trail flattens briefly in a wooded saddle before arcing left (west) into a traverse of a boulder-studded slope. Cross another saddle and begin to descend. At the next saddle, the trail climbs past a couple of switchbacks to the first vista point at 1.2 miles. Climb out onto the overlook rocks and enjoy the views south over the wooded slopes and down east into the sun-stained Carson Valley. You can turn around here, retracing your steps to the trailhead, or go on.

To continue, traverse upward through the forest. Cross a relatively open area, then switch back into the forest. Next, loop around the backside of a knob and stay up, finishing the final upward traverse at the second overlook at 2.0 miles. Again, climb onto the rocks or settle on a flat spot in the shade, and savor the expansive vista to the east. Return as you came; it's all downhill from here.

Option: The next major landmark along the Tahoe Rim Trail as it heads north is Snow Valley Peak, which lies about 3.5 miles north of the second vista point (about 5.5 miles one-way from the trailhead).

18
TAHOE RIM TRAIL SOUTH FROM SPOONER SUMMIT

Type of hike: Out-and-back.

See map on page 60

Total distance: 5 miles.

Elevation gain: 650 feet.

Maps: USGS Glenbrook; USDA Forest Service Lake Tahoe Basin Management Unit Map; Tom Harrison Recreation Map of Lake Tahoe.

Starting point: Spooner Summit trailhead in the Spooner Picnic Area off U.S. Highway 50.

Finding the trailhead: To reach the trailhead from Tahoe City, go north on California 28, which becomes Nevada 28, for 25 miles to the intersection of NV 28 and U.S. Highway 50. Turn left on US 50, and go 0.7 miles to Spooner Summit. Turn right into the picnic area parking lot; there is also parking along US 50.

From the intersection of US 50 and California 89 in South Lake Tahoe, drive north on US 50 for 18 miles to the US 50/NV 28 intersection at the base of Spooner Summit. Follow US 50 an additional 0.7 mile to the summit and trailhead, which is on the right.

Key points:

1.5 Pass a series of saddles.

2.0 Arrive at a sage-covered overlook.

2.5 Cross roadways below Duane Bliss Peak.

The hike: Span a single highway, and marvel at the differences in the terrain. On the north side of Spooner Summit, the Tahoe Rim Trail is relatively easy and well-shaded, with obvious rocky viewpoints. It's not as easy on the south side, where the trail climbs steeply from the trailhead via a series of switchbacks, traversing a rolling ridgeline that offers expansive views of Lake Tahoe to the west and only fleeting views of the sere Carson Valley to the east.

Don't let the switchbacks scare you off, however; the minor difficulties are fleeting and more than mitigated by the mellower hiking that follows and by the sight of Lake Tahoe shimmering through the trees. The lake is especially lovely at dusk. This is also a span of trail that captures the good and bad of forest management, from the vigor of the mixed evergreens that grow on the trail's lower reaches to the scarred landscape and burned stumps of an area that has yet to recover from timber removal.

The trailhead is at the southern border of the picnic area (there is a restroom available here). The trail climbs immediately, with the trademark blue and white signs of the Tahoe Rim Trail marking the route. Switchbacks lead upward and west toward the lake, then back east toward the Carson Valley, eventually reaching a gentle, forested summit where the trail levels, meandering through scruffy pine, mountain hemlock, and mule ear.

More switchbacks follow, leading to a relatively open saddle, then onward and upward again. After cresting the next rise, the trail flattens and actually drops a bit; the traverse features great views southwest across the lake to Mount Tallac and the south shore.

The route rollercoasters through saddles as it spans the ridge at 1.5 miles; each saddle offers respite for the hiker.

As you continue, you will pass a strange pit—perhaps a borrow pit for trail construction—at a scenic curve with views of the lake. At 2.0 miles, ascend onto a lovely sage-covered ridgetop with more awesome views; this too marks a great turnaround or rest stop. Watch for raptors catching updrafts from the basin.

The trail arcs eastward from the summit into an area that has been logged. Exposed patches of red earth, blackened holes where stumps have been burned out, and ragged piles of slash dot the landscape, but if you look carefully, you can see some of the ground squirrels and other small creatures that make the sooty holes their homes. The land is scarred, but nature has already begun reclaiming it.

The trail intersects several four-wheel-drive roads just past the logged area; the sparsely forested slopes of Duane Bliss Peak rise to the east, directly over the route. Cross one of the roads on the Tahoe Rim Trail. The second road dead-ends at 2.5 miles on a small rise with views east over the western reaches of Nevada. The rise is a nice spot for a picnic. This is an ideal turnaround point. Return to the trailhead via the same route.

Options: Though there is no trail, the summit of Duane Bliss Peak is an attractive goal for the intrepid (and experienced) backcountry traveler. Don't attempt this, however, unless you have experience with cross-country routefinding. And, as always, the Tahoe Rim Trail continues south to the Kingsbury Grade and beyond.

19
TAHOE RIM TRAIL
AT BIG MEADOW

Type of hike: Out-and-back.
Total distance: 2 miles.
Elevation gain: 320 feet.
Maps: USGS Freel Peak and Echo Lake; USDA Forest Service Lake Tahoe Basin Management Unit Map; Tom Harrison Recreation Map of Lake Tahoe.
Starting point: Tahoe Rim/Big Meadow trailhead off California 89.
Finding the trailhead: To reach the trailhead from the intersection of U.S. Highway 50 and California 89 in South Lake Tahoe, drive south on US 50/CA 89 for 5.1 miles to the town of Meyers, where the two highways diverge. Go left (southwest) onto CA 89, following it for 5.5 miles to the Big Meadow trailhead. The trailhead parking area is reached via a left (east) turn onto a short access road.

Key points:
0.2 Cross CA 89.
0.7 Reach the edge of the meadow.
1.0 Rest on stumps at turnaround point.

The hike: There is something magical about a mountain meadow. In springtime and early summer wildflowers are the main attraction, vivid in myriad shades of red, purple,

Tahoe Rim Trail at Big Meadow

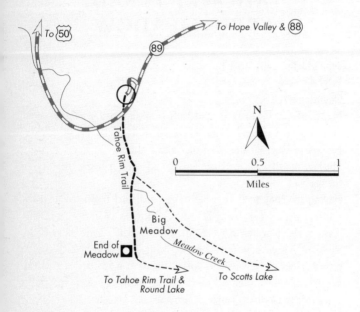

white, and yellow, and busy with butterflies and bees harvesting sweet nectars. By late summer and autumn, the variety of flowers has diminished, but a rich glistening gold has spread over the meadow's expanse; the grasses have absorbed the warm hues of the sun as they have dried and now whisper as the stiffened stalks brush against one another in gentle breezes. Even in winter, blanketed in thick snow, the meadow is a calming, meditative place. Big Meadow is like this, green and gold, easygoing and restful, delightful in all its incarnations.

The Big Meadow hike is the perfect introduction to the seduction of the mountain meadow for the neophyte hiker of any age; it's also wonderfully rejuvenating for the experienced high-country wanderer. A group of stumps at the western edge of the meadow is the perfect place to rest and regroup. And, like buttercream icing on a rich chocolate cake, a river (okay, a gurgling creek) runs through it.

The trail begins at the north edge of the trailhead parking area, just beyond the information sign about the Lahontan cutthroat trout. Pass a blue and white Tahoe Rim Trail sign almost immediately; the trail runs parallel to the highway until it climbs to the edge of the asphalt. Carefully cross the highway at 0.2 mile.

The path steepens on the other side of the roadway, climbing through a forest of stout mixed evergreens. Climb a log staircase that makes it hard to comprehend that mountain bikers often ride the route. At a shadowy trail fork, go left (west) and up, away from the noisy stream.

The trail flattens as the highway noises fade; the boulder-strewn woodland is now full of birdsong and windsong. Pass through the fence via a stile, and continue on the gently ascending track. At the next trail fork go right (northwest), following the arrow that points to Meiss Meadow.

A brief final stretch of woodland, then at 0.7 mile, the world opens into the green (or gold, or white) expanse of the meadow. The trail loops through the grasses, wildflowers, and willows to the proverbial babbling brook, which is spanned by a rustic footbridge. Beyond, the grass encroaches on the route, rendering it soft and quiet as it transects the meadow. Dense forest buffers the edges of the meadow, carpeting the rolling mountains that cradle it.

At 1.0 mile, the trail reaches the interface of the meadow and forest, then plunges on and up into higher country. The sun-bleached logs and stumps rest in the grasses adjacent to the trail; perch on the warm wood and renew your soul, then head back as you came.

Options: From the trail intersection just before you enter the meadow, you can head up and southwest to Scotts Lake, or you can continue on the Tahoe Rim Trail to Round Lake and beyond.

20
WINNEMUCCA LAKE AND ROUND TOP LAKE

Type of hike: Loop.
Total distance: 4.5 miles.
Elevation gain: 1,110 feet.
Maps: USGS Caples Lake and Carson Pass; USDA Forest Service Lake Tahoe Basin Management Unit Map.
Starting point: Winnemucca trailhead at Woods Lake.
Finding the trailhead: To reach the trailhead from the intersection of U.S. Highway 50 and California 89 in South Lake Tahoe, drive south on US 50/CA 89 for 5.1 miles to the town of Meyers, where the two highways diverge. Go left (southwest) onto CA 89, following it for 11.5 miles to its intersection with California 88 in Hope Valley. Go right (northwest) on CA 88, toward Kirkwood and Carson Pass. Drive 11 miles from the CA 89/88 intersection, over the pass, to a left turn on the access road for Woods Lake Campground. Go 1.4 miles on the access road to the trailhead parking area, which is often full; overflow parking is available at spots along the narrow roadway, or in the overflow parking area that you'll pass on your way in.

Key points:
1.5 Reach Winnemucca Lake.
2.2 Rest at Round Top Lake.
3.5 Pass Lost Cabin Mine.

Winnemucca Lake and Round Top Lake

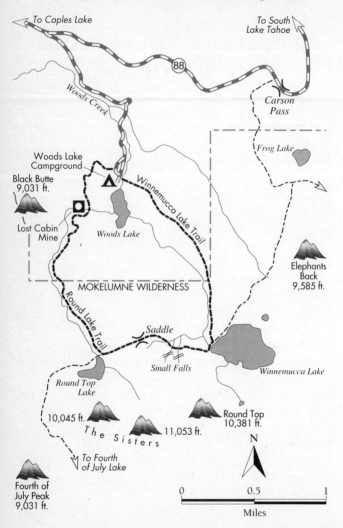

To Caples Lake

To South Lake Tahoe

88

Woods Creek

Carson Pass

Frog Lake

Woods Lake Campground

Black Butte 9,031 ft.

Lost Cabin Mine

Woods Lake

Winnemucca Lake Trail

Elephants Back 9,585 ft.

MOKELUMNE WILDERNESS

Round Lake Trail

Saddle

Small Falls

Winnemucca Lake

Round Top Lake

10,045 ft.

The Sisters

11,053 ft.

Round Top 10,381 ft.

To Fourth of July Lake

Fourth of July Peak 9,031 ft.

N

0   0.5   1

Miles

The hike: In early summer—late June or early July, or when-ever the height of the High Sierran wildflower season oc-curs—this trek should be every Tahoe hiker's highest prior-ity. The northeast-facing hillside that lies below the Winnemucca Lake basin puts on a magnificent wildflower display. The Indian paintbrush alone, in every shade of red from burgundy to antique rose, makes for a scene more than worth the time and effort it takes to view it; this grand flower is accented with purples, yellows, and whites of penstemon and lupine, aster and yarrow, and the vivid green of moun-tain grasses. It's a vision for a painter, not a wordsmith.

Don't miss this hike even if it is not wildflower season. Winnemucca Lake, a perfect alpine tarn friendly to anglers and hikers alike, is a noble and lovely goal; the vistas and seclusion of Round Top Lake only add to this loop's charms. It even boasts a glimpse of the mining legacy so pivotal to California's history in the Lost Cabin Mine, which lies near trail's end.

The trail begins at the Winnemucca trailhead, which is about 100 yards beyond the campground entrance and map and on the left (south) side of the road. Cross the bridge; the trail forks immediately. Go left and up. Climb gently through a mixed evergreen forest dotted with boulders. As you climb, you will cross several seasonal streams and the remains of an "arrastra," a large basinlike structure used by early Mexicans to crush gold and silver-bearing ore rocks.

The forest breaks up and opens onto a wildflower meadow. The trail traverses upward across this slope, gradu-ally steepening as you approach the Winnemucca Lake ba-sin, which is drained by a rollicking stream.

Atop the hillside, you'll reach the trail markers at the shores of Winnemucca Lake at 1.5 miles. The lakeshore lies beyond the second post and invites you to sit and stay a while. The lake sits in a craggy basin where snow lingers into late summer, caught in rocky crevices and shaded by steep cliffs. The wind at timberline can be fierce, as evidenced by the cropped hemlocks that huddle about the shore.

To continue to Round Top Lake, return to the first trail marker and go left (west). Cross the outlet stream before the trail begins to climb. Traverse up across the first small crest, then circle west toward small twin waterfalls that cascade down the steep headwall until the snow that feeds them melts in late summer. Continue up and northwest on the steepening route, climbing into the saddle between the Winnemucca and Round Top basins. Pass through the brief alpine meadow in the gap before dropping down to Round Top Lake and a trail crossing at 2.2 miles.

Kidney-shaped Round Top Lake, its muted green waters set below the sheltering ramparts of the craggy Sisters, is a peaceful place to rest before the descent to Woods Lake. Once you've hoarded a dose of unfiltered sunshine and alpine splendor, return to the trail crossing and go down (north) on the broad easy path, enjoying wonderful views. The trees quickly regain their stature as you drop in altitude; a steep pitch drops you into a willowy wetland interlaced with swift-flowing rivulets.

Pass the Mokelumne Wilderness boundary sign and continue down. The stream grows to a raucous cataract. Eventually, you will cross the stream and bear left (north) past a clearing. Beyond, at 3.5 miles, lie the first straggling signs of the Lost Cabin Mine, including an old metal structure perched on a rock outcrop overlooking the stream, and the remains of an old car that nearly block the trail. Follow the signs to stay on the trail, which bears right (east). Switchbacks lead down past more mining structures to a stream crossing on logs and rocks. A trail sign beyond the vigorous stream keeps you on the Round Top Lake Trail.

Pass the trailhead kiosk, where the trail broadens into a road that lazily curves down past a gate to the campground road; go left (east) to the overflow parking area, and right (west) to the campground proper.

Options: Trails lead to other destinations from both lakes—from Winnemucca Lake to Frog Lake, and from Round Top Lake to Fourth of July Lake. You can avoid the rigors of high-country hiking altogether by staying right just beyond the bridge at the trailhead and walking along the shore of Woods Lake.

21
PACIFIC CREST TRAIL AT ECHO LAKES

Type of hike: One-way with boat taxi shuttle or out-and-back.
Total distance: 2.9 miles or 5.8 miles.
Elevation gain: 100 feet.
Maps: USGS Echo Lakes; USDA Forest Service Lake Tahoe Basin Management Unit Map; Tom Harrison Recreation Map of Lake Tahoe.
Starting point: Pacific Crest trailhead at Echo Chalet.
Finding the trailhead: To reach the Echo Chalet from the intersection of U.S. Highway 50 and California 89 in South Lake Tahoe, drive west on US 50 for 10.2 miles, over Echo Summit, to a right turn onto Johnson Pass Road (with sign). Go 0.6 mile on Johnson Pass Road, heading southeast, to Echo Lakes Road. Turn left on Echo Lakes Road and drive 1.2 miles to the Echo Chalet. Parking can be tight; scout a spot along the road or in the upper parking lot, and walk the short distance down to the chalet and trailhead.

Key points:
2.0 Bridge the gap between the two lakes.
2.9 Reach the boat ramp.

The hike: This stretch of the Pacific Crest Trail traverses from the granite slabs above larger Lower Echo Lake to the forested ramps that shade the Upper Echo Lake. The hiking is

Pacific Crest Trail at Echo Lakes

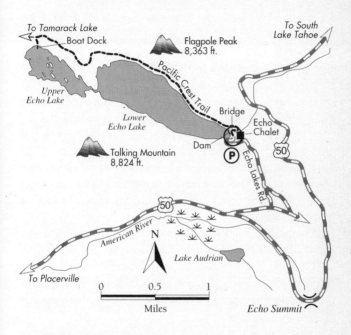

wonderfully easy and visually exciting, especially at the outset, when the route follows a seam in the granite at the base
of Flagpole Peak, which forms the lakes' eastern border. The
surface of the lower lake shimmers in the sun that bathes
the basin; the upper lake is partially hidden by the trees that
shade the small cabins along its shores. Ahead, to the north,
the broad pass between Keiths Dome to the northwest and

Ralston Peak to the southwest rises in a headwall of great silvery terraces, both beckoning and imposing, hinting of the alpine treasures that lie above and beyond.

The trail begins at the southern shore of the lower lake; be sure to fill out a wilderness permit. Walk across the causeway atop the dam and the bridge that spans the spillway. The trail switches back up the hill past the trail signs to the trail intersection. Head left (north) on Pacific Crest Trail, which begins its traverse of the western shores of the lake by climbing through the manzanita onto granite slabs.

The trail is etched in the bleached granite, narrow but well-traveled; it is about 200 feet above the surface of the navy blue water, thrilling with just a touch of exposure. Pass a portion of the trail that has been augmented with asphalt, then around the first of the charming vacation cabins that line both lakes.

Continue along the slabs to a five-foot standing stone; a social path leads onto an overlook.

Beyond, a large rock overhangs the trail, which passes to the right of a storage tank and past a trail sign. Two switchbacks lead up to more traversing toward the northern reaches of the lower lake.

The route drops through a rocky, brushy section in the shadow of an overhanging slab streaked with black, gray, and orange. Pass cabins on the left (west) side of the trail. You'll climb again as you bridge the gap between the two lakes at 2.0 miles; the trail is overhung once again by granite cliffs. As the trail arcs westward, toward the lakes, it is stained orange with iron that has oxidized in the rock.

The trail bends back to the north, traversing a shallow, rocky ravine. Climb out of the gulch to spectacular views of the upper lake and its stony islands. Pass a slab of white rock on the left (west) side of the trail, which offers a nice rest stop, before commencing the gentle traverse along the wooded shores of the upper lake. As you proceed, views of the lake are lost amid the dense forest, with its colorful understory of brush, grass, and wildflowers. A series of small, stone-lined culverts cross the seasonal streams that water the forest floor.

Crest a small hill with shady views. At the big fir tree, you'll see a narrow path that branches off to the left (west). Just beyond is another leftward trail; this one has a sign high on a tree that reads "Public phone and boat launch." Take either route about 50 yards down to the boat dock at 2.9 miles, where indeed there is a public phone in a little hut to the north.

Options: You have three choices at this point. You can enjoy the ambiance of the shores of the upper lake before returning the way you came. Or you can wait on the launch for the boat taxi from Echo Chalet; this arrives every half-hour or less during the summer and offers a wonderful boat ride back to the trailhead for a moderate fee (the perfect option for families). Or you can avoid the boat launch altogether, continuing onward and upward into the high country, where a wonderland of lakes, including grand Lake Aloha, awaits. Wilderness permits are required for those continuing into higher country.

22
HORSETAIL FALLS

Type of hike: Out-and-back.
Total distance: 2.4 miles.
Elevation gain: 440 feet.
Maps: USGS Echo Lakes; USDA Forest Service Lake Tahoe Basin Management Unit Map; Tom Harrison Recreation Map of Lake Tahoe.
Starting point: Twin Bridges trailhead.
Finding the trailhead: To reach Twin Bridges from the intersection of U.S. Highway 50 and California 89 in South Lake Tahoe, drive west on US 50 for 16 miles, over Echo Summit, to the parking lot on the right (northeast) side of the road just before the bridge at Twin Bridges.

Key points:
0.5 Climb the first granite slabs.
1.2 Reach the slab overlooking the falls.

The hike: Horsetail Falls is a spectacular sight. The snowy cascade, spilling from cliffs that form the eastward rampart of a narrowing valley, beckons from the grand granite slabs of the trail, from the clear pools of Pyramid Creek, which skitters toward and away from the trail as it ascends, even from the dusty parking area and the noisy highway at the trailhead.

Horsetail Falls

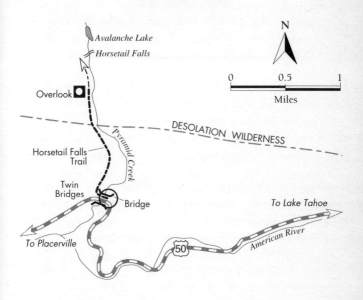

The falls themselves are not easy to reach, because the trail, though clear at outset, becomes a more difficult cross-country route the closer you get to the base of the cascade. Continue through the canyon only if you have good route-finding tools and experience, and abundant energy. The route I describe here is not that ambitious; it ends on a sunbaked slab with views of the falls and the surrounding valley. Regardless of the final destination, this route requires that you use caution and common sense. The trail can be hard to follow as it crosses blank slabs and winds through forest amid a series of social trails; you may find that you temporarily lose it either on the ascent or descent. Fortunately, other hikers frequent the path, and Pyramid Creek can be used as a homing beacon; you can follow it downstream (southwest) toward the highway until you intersect the trail. It is virtually impossible to get lost.

The trail begins on the opposite side of the bridge from the parking area. Walk alongside the road over the bridge, past the Twin Bridges sign, to where the highway railing ends. Go right onto the trail, which is marked and bears northeast. Walk up and over the first slabs and into the woods; the vigorous clamor of the trailside stream soon overwhelms the highway noise.

Strategically placed stones allow easy crossing of the seasonal streamlets that feed the creek. The trail leaves the woods at the base of a short slab headwall and goes slightly left across the rolling slab, staying left of the naked signpost. There are several ways to reach the top of the slabs; I followed a set of large granite stairs to the base of a broad, black-streaked fold in the slab, then stayed right, skirting the edge of the slab, to its crest at 0.5 mile. Any route will do; the broad, sandy trail becomes obvious on top of the slab. It continues climbing through scrub and jumbled stones with the falls clearly in its sights.

Cross sand and granite slabs as you continue on relatively flat terrain. The creek is briefly divorced from the route, lying below and to the right (southeast) of the slabs on which the trail lies. It will run alongside the trail again by the time you reach the Desolation Wilderness sign, where you must fill out the wilderness permit form.

Beyond, the trail enters forest shade, and beautiful clear pools surrounded by sunny slabs invite rest. A cairn marks the end of yet another slab crossing; beyond, the trail enters a glade of fir and hemlock. Cross two seasonal streams and stay left at the small trail crossings. More cairns mark passage over yet another slab, from which you have a brief vista of the falls. At 1.2 miles, the trail skirts the base of a large sloping rock platform. Scramble up onto this platform for views of the falls, a noisy spillway scouring cliff walls that bear a scanty covering of evergreens and scrub. Absorb some sunshine and peace—and perhaps a picnic—before heading back as you came.

Option: The trail continues streamside from the base of the large rock slabs, but it becomes ever more rustic, overgrown, and difficult to discern as you ascend toward the base of the falls. This is recommended only to more experienced hikers, and is not recommended for hikers carrying backpacks.

About the Author

Tracy Salcedo has been a writer and outdoors enthusiast for most of her life. She is the author of a number of hiking guidebooks to Colorado, where she lived for 12 years. In addition, she has written numerous articles on hiking, mountain biking and skiing for newspapers and several national magazines. She currently resides in California's Wine Country, where, in the company of her husband and three sons, she continues to write and participate in a variety of outdoor pursuits.

get
FALCON GUIDED

All books in this popular series are regularly updated with accurate information on access, side trips, & safety.

HIKING GUIDES

Hiking Alaska
Hiking Alberta
Hiking Arizona
Hiking Arizona's Catcus Country
Hiking the Beartooths
Hiking Big Bend National Park
Hiking California
Hiking California's Desert Parks
Hiking Carlsbad Caverns &
   Guadalupe Mnts. National Parks
Hiking Colorado
Hiking the Columbia River Gorge
Hiking Florida
Hiking Georgia
Hiking Glacier/Waterton Lakes
Hiking Grand Canyon National Park
Hiking Grand Staircase-Escalante
Hiking Great Basin
Hiking Hot Springs in the Pacific NW
Hiking Idaho
Hiking Maine
Hiking Michigan
Hiking Minnesota
Hiking Montana
Hiking Nevada
Hiking New Hampshire
Hiking New Mexico
Hiking New York
Hiking North Carolina
Hiking North Cascades
Hiking Northern Arizona
Hiking Olympic National Park
Hiking Oregon

Hiking Oregon's Eagle Cap Wilderness
Hiking Oregon's Mt Hood/Badger Creek
Hiking Oregon's Three Sisters Country
Hiking Pennsylvania
Hiking Shenandoah National Park
Hiking South Carolina
Hiking South Dakota's Black Hills Cntry
Hiking Southern New England
Hiking Tennessee
Hiking Texas
Hiking Utah
Hiking Utah's Summits
Hiking Vermont
Hiking Virginia
Hiking Washington
Hiking Wyoming
Hiking Wyoming's Wind River Range
Hiking Yellowstone National Park
Hiking Zion & Bryce Canyon
Exploring Canyonlands & Arches
The Trail Guide to Bob Marshall Cntry

BEST EASY DAY HIKES

Beartooths
Canyonlands & Arches
Glacier & Waterton Lakes
Grand Staircase-Escalante/Glen Cny
Grand Canyon
North Cascades
Olympics
Shenandoah
Yellowstone

FALCON®

MORE THAN 5 MILLION COPIES SOLD!

get
FALCON GUIDED

PADDLING GUIDES

Floater's Guide to Colorado
Paddling Montana
Paddling Okeefenokee
Paddling Oregon
Paddling Yellowstone/Grand Teton

ROCK CLIMBING GUIDES

Rock Climbing Colorado
Rock Climbing Montana
Rock Climbing New Mexico & Texas
Rock Climbing Utah

ROCKHOUNDING GUIDES

Rockhounding Arizona
Rockhound's Guide to California
Rockhound's Guide to Colorado
Rockhounding Montana
Rockhounding Nevada
Rockhound's Guide to New Mexico
Rockhounding Texas
Rockhounding Utah
Rockhounding Wyoming

BIRDING GUIDES

Birding Minnesota
Birding Montana
Birding Texas
Birding Utah

FIELD GUIDES

Canyon Country Wildflowers
Great Lakes Berry Book
New England Berry Book
Pacific Northwest Berry Book
Plants of Arizona
Rare Plants of Colorado
Rocky Mountain Berry Book
Tallgrass Prairie Wildflowers
Western Trees
Wildflowers of Southwestern Utah
Willow Bark and Rosehips

WALKING

Walking Colorado Springs
Walking Denver
Walking Portland
Walking St. Louis

FISHING GUIDES

Fishing Alaska
Fishing the Beartooths
Fishing Florida
Fishing Glacier
Fishing Maine
Fishing Michigan
Fishing Montana
Fishing Wyoming
Fishing Yellowstone

To order check with you local bookseller or
call FALCON® at **1-800-582-2665**.
www.falconguide.com

FALCON®

get
FALCON GUIDED

SCENIC DRIVING GUIDES

WILDLIFE VIEWING GUIDES

FALCON®

get FALCON GUIDED

MOUNTAIN BIKING GUIDES

Mountain Biking Arizona
Mountain Biking Colorado
Mountain Biking Georgia
Mountain Biking New Mexico
Mountain Biking New York
Mountain Biking N. New England
Mountain Biking Oregon
Mountain Biking South Carolina
Mountain Biking S. New England
Mountain Biking Utah
Mountain Biking Wisconsin

LOCAL CYCLING SERIES

Bend
Boise
Bozeman
Chequamegon
Colorado Springs
Denver/Boulder
Durango
Helena
Moab
White Mountains (West)

BIRDING GUIDES

Birding Minnesota
Birding Montana
Birding Texas
Birding Utah

PADDLING GUIDES

Floater's Guide to Colorado
Paddling Montana
Paddling Okeefenokee
Paddling Oregon
Paddling Yellowstone/Grand Teton

ROCKHOUNDING GUIDES

Rockhounding Arizona
Rockhound's Guide to California
Rockhound's Guide to Colorado
Rockhounding Montana
Rockhounding Nevada
Rockhound's Guide to New Mexico
Rockhounding Texas
Rockhounding Utah
Rockhounding Wyoming

FISHING GUIDES

Fishing Alaska
Fishing Beartooths
Fishing Florida
Fishing Glacier
Fishing Maine
Fishing Montana
Fishing Wyoming
Fishing Yellowstone

To order check with you local bookseller or
call FALCON* at **1-800-582-2665**.

www.falconguide.com

FALCON®